Also in this collection:

Going to Seed:
Essays on Idleness, Nature, and Sustainable Work
by Kate J. Neville

Birds at Night

POEMS

IBE LIEBENBERG

TEXAS TECH UNIVERSITY PRESS

This book is typeset in Adobe Caslon Pro. The paper used in this book meets the minimum requirements of ANSI/NISO Z39.48-1992 (R1997). ♾

Designed by Hannah Gaskamp
Cover design by Hannah Gaskamp

Library of Congress Cataloging-in-Publication Data

Names: Liebenberg, Ibe, author. Title: Birds at Night: Poems / Ibe Liebenberg. Other titles: Birds at Night (Compilation)
Description: Lubbock, Texas: Texas Tech University Press, 2025. | Summary: "A poetry collection exploring themes of loss, trauma, PTSD, indigeneity, and familial relationships"—Provided by publisher.
Identifiers: LCCN 2024058086 | ISBN 978-1-68283-251-6 (paperback)
Subjects: LCGFT: Poetry.
Classification: LCC PS3612.I3278 B57 2025 | DDC 811/.6—dc23/eng/20241212
LC record available at https://lccn.loc.gov/2024058086

Texas Tech University Press
Box 41037
Lubbock, Texas 79409-1037 USA
800.832.4042
ttup@ttu.edu

www.ttupress.org

To Allie, Mona, and Lucy

Contents

Birds at Night

Certain Streets

a firefighter will not go

One is marked with flowers.
I do not drive down that street
or any of the others.
They put up pictures and crosses
to remind me to look away.

Some have nothing
because I pave over them in sleep.
Set up signs, do not enter,
closed forever.

If I forget, or am
forced to revisit,
I will look ahead,
stare at the center line,
unfocus my eyes and
make a memory to believe.
Tell myself I saved you.

doing cpr on some dude who looks
just like my father

and he has been dead so many years
i barely recognize him

but for him   i could fake that heart
into beating   a few more times

of compressions
i'd breathe for him

press my lips into his
even though it is against protocol

ribs give under weight
i fall through

thirty one shitty   thirty two beautiful
reunited minutes   i lose count

in the chaos of the body
i barely knew him anyway

            in the ambulance
            my hands consent

to skin becoming cold
arms practice pushing away

at the hospital
they cannot separate us

so i apologize for the violence
of not letting go

PTSD

it is 2am ugly,
beautiful is sleeping.

and body parts   are now religion.

a holy cult
where the angels won't shut up

about our weeping.
all over the road,
        your chalk outline,

limb-scattered vessel,
a temporary home.

i bring it to the station
resurrect you
night into night.

trace the white scribbled shape
                    into a body.

in my room
the ghosts unfold me,

caress my uniform
before putting it on.

and when the angels do not see us,
wings undressed; they leave.

we are the frowns of your absence,
ghosts holding up our clothes.

The Few Times I Have Cried

Not for my father's funeral.

When that friend died at seventeen.

I was laid off from work when we were already bruised. Every job offer was half the pay. I worked eighty hours each week to try to find the way back from fragile.

You said we would be okay.

That night, while you were all asleep, I paused at the car door before leaving for work
to listen to geese labor through a no moon, starred dark. A few clouds dizzied our distance.
Their wings coughed out cold sky. I worried about you and the kids, and whether the car I stood next to would be repossessed in the parking lot of my work while I posed inside.

Walking outside work to see the car gone.

The walk home.

About feeding our kids.

About you leaving.

That night, standing outside the car, after the birds had gone, we became cloud, then rain. And those birds.

Those birds flying at night. The wrong way through winter.

Wolf OR-93

it was hunger. not the lust i imagined.
or the wasted no-shame howl. you sang.

your leg shattered.
on the side of the road. a cemetery.

                         a ghost
sorrowing through grass in winter.

i read about you on the news.
wondered how to calculate lonely.
what level would you be. besides the highest.
                   not hunger. not love.

i am still measuring the word.

Cousin Wolf Sings

Her all-night melody blushes
like directions for new lovers
            who are lost.

Last night all she held was a hum
            that ran away.

She now stretches words in our broken-down car

somewhere on Valley View
between Orphaned Lane
            and the dead end,

about hidden roads and streets
of homes for all the abandoned.

I study the map when she falls from crescendo.

Flashlight held by my teeth,
her voice needs
both hands to trace.

She leads me down paths disappearing
into blue lines holding
            imaginary rivers,

blacking in thin creases
and folds or contoured lines.

She drones about the water. I find the blue again.
My hand pressed against
            the faded shore.

Junky Brother Blues

I collect his birthdays like they are
                         my hands
rubbing together empty

break them open   simple as winter
shaky   like earth searching
for her vacant moon

these days are bare skin
trees and snow embraced
           underneath

at night   I stitch cold into blankets
                 to walk on

the streets cough out

stiff as newborn lungs
before the slap open

don't bring your 6-year-old daughter to a wild horse
auction, just bring a horse home

she will trace the shapes of scars
ask where each one came from
                              why are they called wild?
she will try to release each one
only after naming them   *thunder*
                                cloud
and the one called   *poorly drawn stars*
is the one she chooses

then asks about freeze marks
the burn to remove freedom

she will tame our gaze on raised skin
and the brand flinching

discipline refusing body
the wild not giving in

Birds at Night

Overhead,
under tired silhouettes,
fighting through the almost dark,
wings touching black,
the blur between stars disappears.
The sound of labor and pain
against the earth
and sky not caring.

why i never put *rez* or *off rez* on my resume

or that I was born on *ceremonial land*
because the shitty out of state *off rez* free healthcare
made my body   a cavity
flinch when hurts

they told me

to California   you are   *at will*
to my chickasaw   *at large*
to me   an anonymous song

while we were quiet

i wanted those hips that rose heavy
and waist skinny to bloom

she only swole to a curse
called my body sterile

doctors promised she was barren

teach me how to say it
words that numb

how to sedate a space
when a mother or child provoke
and harass her

help me gentle the room
so I can soften

and balance a flood
to a silly commotion

then pretend her back home
messy in our bed
like the labor she wished for

Taking Care of Mother

I brush her hair
        like I have nothing else to do.
She thinks I am her father.

Maybe he slowly worked his way through tangles
not to make her head pull back.
Bought a special brush that claimed
to not get caught in unkept hair.

I was told
I would get my ears pulled
        to make me cry
and when I wouldn't,
        she would slap me.

It was something about not making sound
that scared her.

My sister died before I was born,
        only months old.

And I
silent child
refused to cry.

        She held me
there worried   awake
        not letting me sleep.

PTSD: *A firefighter's lamentation*

They do not wander off,
walk around lost,
or even get up from the ground
to search for loved ones.

There is no floating away
into the sky
with gilded wings
to embrace heaven.

Instead,
eyes open
or closed,
they stay here
with me.

it's always three in the morning

of compressions
    breathe

for him   fake a heart
into beating one more time

ribs give under weight
    i fall through

thirty one hush   thirty two quiet
minutes   i lose count

at the station
in my room
i calculate loss
    like anyone
a fugitive to sleeping

This Is Paradise

After the Camp Fire

Trees that survived
will be taken next.
They have suffered so much.
I see sky now,
birds that look lost.
People glare like
we do not belong.

Our engine
presses a lovely red hue
like a flower against
the burned earth.
We drive down streets
no longer named,
act surprised
when we are lost.

Origin Story

could have been raven
scraping her beak
against granite sparking

or dipping crane
stirring death
from waters dumb

floated mush on surface
we circulate to shore
gather sticks that coil like serpents

first words peck
and slobber from mouths
lowered heads shake out wild
closed eyes become worship

Ceremony

Pace the table scratches and inked boredom
of my youth. I am responsible for all of it.

When I tried to ignore her, I was impossible.
There is a word in Chickasaw for you, she said.

Chepota loma   the *bastard*. I didn't think
I existed. The word existed. In that other tongue.

A wobble in the uneven of oak chair.
An auntie stables behind me.

Other family lean in too.
We posture the pause.

She could birth the words for being fatherless
to me again. Walked away from.

My hands clamp the chair,
wait to be called something with my wandering stutter

I call accent. A name that will stain until her death
or we declare she is her own disaster.

Things They Want After Fire

to the dog I found under a bed

Hands offer
compressions

to swollen body.
Mouth around

blackened nose
expires. The taste

of failure stains
the hole dug

beside a tree for you.
At the station,

in my room
I shovel through sleep.

Like a bad obituary,
plagiarize me better.

Please let my mouth pronounce these words

my first Chickasaw lesson

tell me speak better
to articulate   dumb child
these big lips honey together
        the labor

I don't know my accent grandmother

mouth open and busy
hurrying her language to me
        an-nun-ci-ate your words
Anowa   for   *again*
her syllables bruise apart

between words I rest

                without flinch

she inhales—   wild bees
gather the sting

Growing up Coyote in the Wolf Clan

All night the buzz of complaining lights
                              keeps us employed.

Our days are the drain
and water circling.

           From the foreign places we feel labor,
                    work being done.

Cousin wolf sings about pawning love
          like it is inheritance.

A song for any sweet or stealing thing

she is soliciting. Last night
                    all she had was a hum

for us runaways. Tonight, she sings in our car

about finding hidden roads
and streets of homes for the abandoned.

Together with Tears

It was a day trip for her
and her friends.
She told me about walking
a mile or so of the Trail of Tears.
Mentioned how slow they moved,
even cried.

I wondered how much she knew.
If she even understood why they stopped
each time on the path.
Not to rest because they're tired or hungry,
but only to bury their dead.
And not one by one,
but together.
Not to stop every time someone fell.
Not to bury anyone alone,
but to bury together.

Anthesis

My definition of sadness: *imagine I am smiling.*

The only picture of my dad surrendered to a load of laundry.

Found his obituary online, read it like a stranger would.

A resume of people who loved him.

I move through wet clothes to feel the pieces, of course,

cry, but love is a flower that does not care

who watches him bloom.

Stepfather Number One

His hands easy, please.
Know the posture,

embarrassed position
I still bend to. Whispers,

maybe prayer, or just his lips tightened
to a smile. I never knew,

or wanted our eyes introduced
formally. He wouldn't stop until he could

see my body harden
and stomached breath held.

Bodies have a way
of betraying. I wish

I could have cried easy,
like in movies. Fake

my way through the scene.
My definition of *crying*: Not tears,

just awful noise. I can still hear
the ridiculous sound.

Upon Finding a Picture of My Estranged Father Holding Me

There I am
in the February sun,
feeling his gaze.
I look only days old.

The winter,
shadowed behind
his shirtless body,
cradles me in uncertainty.
He shields me from cold.

This is what
a father feels like.
He once held me,
wrapped in smile.

Stepfather Number Two

wanted to cut down the dead
oak in the back that housed
the vultures. Said it was dangerous
above his barn. They rest there every night
and on clouded mornings were held
                              for me, wings open

to the direction of sun. In that dead tree
I waited for leaves. I saw
happiness. I saw everything. But

no one noticed on each of his pills
the word *forever*. The highest stage of depression.
                      His oak above the barn.
                      To rest. To warm.
                      The way off earth when cloudy.

Accents

I can't hear the hiss of accents
The tongue unstressed anymore.
Mom yells with stepfather one.
It is just words, all of it stressing.
In class I am asked to listen
to the line. To hear
each measure as if not shouting.
When I speak, it is all mess on my lips.
And while the belt is raised, I am told
love should be quiet and useful,
with the warmth of leather
on the living room floor.

Deadbeat Dad

It has been a sloppy celibacy. To be honest
an unfair exchange. Nothing to pawn
but the unpaid bills of our marriage.

I have not heard from our son
in six months, between us, it has started to rain.
He must be doing fine.

He would have called. To need me.
Is it so bad to want something minimal to happen?
I have called seventeen times

just to know I am not blocked.
Like a slow deflating tire, I drive on,
then realize I never showed him how

to change a flat. But he would
have a friend there. I text
every day, then call someone obscene,

and she responds. I just need to know
the earth still wobbles, and the moon
pulls you lopsided, not me.

CPR @ 2pm

I have rehearsed all of this.
The physical emotion.
I've closed eyes. Drowned
the room crying. I was the breathless
walls. The stress of sirens and
engine cussing residence.
I was the finger shaking the map
and the road to your house trembling.

I did not practice the neighborhood scream.
The buzzing single-wide florescent light.
I did not practice a blue doll left alone
on the living room floor. I never practiced
no one holding you.

Why I Love Lame Excuses from College Freshmen

I hate it when their dads die
their moms too
but dad always dies more
so I relate
trying to sit through class
with your bones not there to support you
you dissolve into the desk
try to disappear
just tell me your alarm did not wake you
pull yourself together
and forget what day it was
like I did
when my dad died

Memorial Day

naked ladies' surface
in the beds
outside the church
the only flowers
for his wake

dad is with me
in the car
for the first time
mom cradles him
in the small box

are we to unbury
without direction
throw his dust
at random

cliff wind evaporates
him into ocean
sea-ash-sky-blue
becomes color
knees thaw to grass
I soften to the field

Witness

They stand around
while I compress
her chest   violent.
Watch their naked   neighbor
out of indecency.

There is a lightning fire
in Siskiyou County   growing.
We will probably leave at three a.m.
to be the fresh crew
for the twenty-four-hour shift that
becomes thirty-six.

feather river canyon

almost threw my rope to water
pretending to be the child
a small shirt waving sleeves
was too much body

i am lonely on the shore
waiting hours in rain
the boy shirtless wherever he is
will return

while the river gossips
then argues with me
a burial as if agreeing
the high water mark sign nods

above our engines
at the station in my room
i slip into the water
resurrect the hours

before his family drove
from the road
hours before
their recovery

On the Way to and from a Vehicle Rollover with Ejection

Lights flash,
bounce off trees,
red, then yellow.
The rhythm nauseates,
coupled with the siren polluting the air,
we are apocalypse.

And I am powerless
to recreate the moment before
she rested on the ground.
I leave myself there broken.

How to Kill Your Brother

I said bi
          but he heard something else
and leaned away

creating space

no longer in orbit together
          that lean
like being anything
                    but straight
          is bent or broken
          becomes forever

same word in chickasaw for wolf and coyote

so, my brother nashoba calls me

ofi, the dog

spirit wrong

half wolf, half coyote.

says he would still call me dog

if i was all coyote, even

if mother nashoba made me full wolf

he said i would be wolf artificial.

a stray handful of fur from my neck

in his grip.

Litany of things I don't mind

His hands that never touched me.
The way she laughs after being obscene. First
Sunrise on open water. Lost at sea. Dying
When it is needed. The way my dog looks at me
when I forget to roll down her window.
To be ruined. To be burned.
I was a pathetic mess, how easy, this mess.

Donating my body to a figure drawing class

Cross my legs
if you need to
        gaze unaroused.

I thought that is why
I was here.

Make me thick
        and animal.
Veins on my arms
elicited from page.

Unblush this face.
Take my smile as penance.

I could wear a collared shirt
or prude me into a tie.

Dislocate what you need
to loosen me
for a beat.

Open a hand for dance then
        float over this paper
like a ghost
go slow through me.

mouth to mouth, baby bird me

what isn't rent anymore
the unpaid

lights and water flinching cold
through these walls

and under heavy blankets
we spark, we glisten together

to watch our half naked bodies
run outside

and grin with each fire we smother

Last Night Was a Miscarriage

She sits in the middle of our planter holding
weeds and everything that will not flower.

My seven-year-old peony
survived three moves, divorce,
and was my only possession from the fire,

sprouted to the pile of broken. And god help me
and everything that does not bloom.

Because her smile
translates her face
through a suffering glow.

Facing South

I still go back some days
to see them bloom
the flowers that we planted

Maybe I just miss you
and how you randomly placed flowers in
places, I would later move.

I can still hold your hand
in that space around the roots.
We both laughed that they
were buried in dirt.
You smiled and couldn't stop talking
about how good the sun felt. I wanted to
take a picture but you said you looked
awful. We had no idea what we were doing.

Blankets and Bones

Chickasaw Migration Story

The pole leans toward a rising sun
and another day of walking.
The warm glow has not yet topped the trees
and my legs are already tired.
Woman with child
And the others too small,
So I carry one and our belongings.
Blankets and the bones
Of my mother and son tied
To my back hold me together.
Our rest is beyond each step
And a new home every morning.

gar fish dance

spread fingers to mouth
make fangs. shake out

shelled rhythms to songs.
hand tight deer skins
                  become drum.

we dizzy on flesh all summer.
dance at it. spin around.

wear teeth   like hands held
around our necks. a protection.

Bounty

Five Dollars for Every Chicken Hawk, circa 1926

Nothing but liability floats alone.
Not wings ownership of sky
or feathers checkered patterns
to make hens scatter.
You are five dollars
waveless and broken.
You are a clear sky ceremony.

half staff

these flowers underneath

                    winter orphans

still buried lilies we gather

        about why you did it
        flag and pole coupled close

we say we cannot

                understand

Patience

In the Museum of Destruction and Human Everything
in downtown Fort Bragg, California I search
                    for the self-destruct button.

I have waited in a parking lot
in Williams, California for a fire
to happen. It was not romantic,
                    a purgatory view,
estranged birds falling.

I lost my wife because————
her name was Patience.

She was not shot,
but felt bullet-holed,
stapled then sewn, they say
                    surgery was indecent,
an efficient surrender.

It was peaceful and deliberate
in the waiting room. Waiting.

Structure Fire @ 2am

Our alarm is fist to chest, opened
                    hands slap
my head. Paradise, long pause,
structure, pause, 258 whatever road.
I write all of this down,
struggle with clothes,
the engine,   more clothes,
the map,   the house,
we are there,
three half-woke jezebels
falling. Inside an evacuation,
        mess and reckless,
        sleep, desperate to
get these dogs off us.

dear body,

we are smoke, breath lazy. what disappointment.
we should've died this summer.

i was always told to have red around
me. fire and body. ash sedated landscape.

tired. as the air tanker paints our body. canvas.

Fire Season 2015

Give her everything,
I think I will survive.
The sun coughs me out
onto a hillside smoldering.

Our account is overdrawn,
she texts me. I'm melting
and salted through
to the back of my shirt.

I am not a yellow flower
but a stain on a mountain.
It is day forty straight
and we were on this land last summer.

I remember when fan blades were metal
and the guard was wide
enough to fit a hand through,
but you didn't care.

Fire Season 2016

You could be gone all summer
while your family forgets. They recognize
the paychecks you send. She produces
the loops and uncertainty of your signature,
measures the worth of your name
then scribbles it.

      You are calculated in miles
      away, then in days. She files paperwork
      and asks what fire is it, so they can find and serve
      you. You, reduced to participating transient,
      as they continue to remember
      you all wrong. Not as a flower on a hillside, wanting
      your mother to find you this way.

These miles.

Statue

Gabriel said,
It will be heavy.
I can only assume he meant pain.
The feeling of missing someone forever,
and not his frozen image held in
the feminized stone angel holding out hands
above mother's grave.
I cannot unfocus on the wings.
The shadowed underside
casting shade on flowers I carefully planted
that need sun. And
I don't know if he is landing
or leaving to heaven empty handed.

As She Falls Apart

Cancer set traps
To save feral kittens
She wakes early to wake me
Check them
Bring them food
Whispers *get up* in my ear
It is dark out and I am sleeping
And she is not angel enough yet
To lift me from dreams
Where this ends spectacular

There Are Feathers on Our Flag

she was released

to us in bags of ash.
this is what you paid for.
poor people. poor child.

here are your clouds forever.

my hawk shakes gravity.
gives feathers for our flag.

stomachs the wind
we don't want to.

birds at night

the harass of quiet
wings gathering

over the hush
of their dark
magnified

is midnight
full of loud bodies

the geese lost
now
circling one a.m.
above the trees

my elders say
it is a gift to translate
these unspeakable things
all I hear is

real labor

          real pain

in whatever tongue
they sing

Previous Publication Venues

Action, Spectacle: "half staff" and "feather river canyon"

The American Journal of Poetry: "Patience" and "The Few Times I Have Cried"

Beloit Poetry Journal: "Fire Season 2015" and "Fire Season 2016"

Blackbird: "PTSD," "Ceremony," "CPR @ 2pm," and "don't bring your 6-year-old daughter"

Blue River Review (Creighton University, Nebraska): "Birds at Night" and "Together with Tears"

Columbia Granger's World of Poetry: "Cousin Wolf Sings" and "same word in chickasaw for wolf and coyote" (republished from *Poetry Magazine*, forthcoming)

Ecotone: "why i never put *rez* or *off rez* on my resume" and "Wolf OR-93"

HAIS: A Literary Journal: "Taking Care of Mother," "Memorial Day," "How to Kill Your Brother," and "Facing South"

IAIA Student Anthology: "Litany of things I don't mind"

Journal of Chickasaw History and Culture: "Blankets and Bones"

The Lake: "Anthesis"

Prometheus Dreaming: "Certain Streets"

Passaic / Völuspá: "This Is Paradise"

Poetica Publishing: Mizmor Anthology 2019, "Statue"

POETRY Magazine: "Cousin Wolf Sings," "same word in chickasaw for wolf and coyote," and "it's always three in the morning"

Poetry Northwest: "while we were quiet" and "birds at night"

Salamander Magazine: "Origin Story"

Serendipity: Special Edition Chapbook (Black Lesbian Literary

Collective): "Upon Finding a Picture of My Estranged Father Holding Me"

Sugar House Review: "Please let my mouth pronounce these words" and "Things They Want After Fire"

The Threepenny Review: "Donating my body to a figure drawing class," "PTSD: *A firefighter's lamentation*," "Why I Love Lame Excuses from College Freshmen," "Junky Brother Blues," "Last Night Was a Miscarriage," and "doing cpr on some dude who looks just like my father"

Verse Daily: "why i never put *rez* or *off rez* on my resume" (republished from *Ecotone*)

Awards and Nominations

Tribal College Journal Student Creative Contest winner (2023), "gar fish dance"

Poetry Northwest, James Welch Poetry Contest finalists (2023), "while we were quiet" and "birds at night"

About the Author

Ibe Liebenberg is an enrolled citizen of the Chickasaw Nation. He lives in Chico, California, and works as a firefighter for the state and lecturer at Chico State University. He has an MFA from the Institute of American Indian Arts (IAIA) in poetry and fiction. He has been published in *Poetry* magazine, *The Threepenny Review*, and many other venues.

www.ingramcontent.com/pod-product-compliance
Lightning Source LLC
Chambersburg PA
CBHW031659130225
21904CB00005B/509